YAS

Printed in the United States of America

Coleman'

ISBN: 978-0-692-04881-8

First printing, 2018

Cori D. Coleman

You've already started

By Christian Cole

<u>TABLE OF CONTENTS</u>

Introduction

Listen, this isn't the 300 page novel about ups and downs. Neither is this the self-help "Your life can change," novel. No, and in fact, this is actually the one thing you are going to be happy you read before those books.

What do you want to do?

Well I have news for you, before you answered that question you were already doing it. You already are doing it. So many people question the "American way" which would be an honest living by chasing one's dreams. Incredibly true. However, I'm not about to prepare you for a life journey. Instead, I am going to keep it short and sweet.
Your life has been struggle and frustration. Mines is struggle and frustration, so I know. However, you think to yourself, "My life could be a book."

Well, it could be, but will it be? The information I am about to share to you is so small but so powerful. It is secrets, and information people would charge you hundreds of dollars for and I am giving it to you for $1. And maybe some tax included but nonetheless this is a steal.

This will not read like any ordinary book. Because, and you should never start a sentence with because, it is no ordinary book. This book is the reason you will make it as an author, or you will not. Either way, I am giving you a fair shot.

In this book is information editors will wish you were never told. Publishers are going to cringe and wish you'd stop pursuing this foolish dream. Well, they can wish all they want. You have the information now and it is time to use it. I promise you nothing in this book does not work. It all works. The only thing you have to do is supply yourself with confidence and money. Yes, money is the root of all goodness. It takes money to make money. Or maybe you just want your story told. Still takes money and nothing more than that. Lucky for you, I feel like spilling all the dirty little secrets.

<u>All you need to know</u>

Dear Reader,

  First, I want to congratulate you on beginning your journey. Most people want to write but truly never initiate the first step.

  Next, get a notepad because you are going to be reading for a while.

So, if I am correct you have already started writing. Good news is that you are already on your way. I tell many aspiring writers that you have to write. And, I mean write a lot.
However, if you have not started writing do not panic, it is easy.

Just write!

It will come to you, the good and the bad. But you have to start. Trust me, just write. Thomas Edison made the light bulb work on his 201st attempt. Now, in 200 attempts you should know by then if writing is something you are naturally good at or, you need to do some research.

Now everyone offers writing workshops, blah blah. Listen to me, Google exist. Google is your friend and you must trust Google like Rose trusted Jack on the Titanic. You stop buying what you can learn. Want to edit? There are editors with so many articles teaching you for FREE! Want to improve on your scene description? Well, if I had a dollar for every article on how to create a scene in a novel, well I'd be filthy almost rich. There aren't that many articles but there are enough. Either way you see where I am going - Google it!

Next thing you might consider is **research**.

Ask yourself these questions:

• what kind of novel/book am I writing?

- What is my story about and what makes it unique?
- How will my book differ from other books in its genre?

SYNOPSIS

A what? This is the beginning to end rundown of how your story will play out. The synopsis needs to be so enticing that as you read through you feel the irreversible desire to actually go read the book. When composing a synopsis you want to have strong sentences that detail but not over pour.

These are questions you need to answer. The answers to these questions will help you develop your project. Before I write, however, I do one of few things. And that is what I am about to share with you. Sit tight.

The Process

1. Format

Lay your story out. Determine your protagonist,
and then determine their conflict. After you have both,
next you can figure out what their story is. By knowing
what information you need to describe your character,
you will offer yourself a new route of research. Think
about the story you are telling and is it for self or will it
be for others. Many authors write stories assuming the
world wants to know their story. Sometimes, not so
much. Focus on what makes your story so compelling.

Now, let's say you are writing a self-help book.
Never and I repeat never write a book about self-help
describing your life and how what you went through
helped you. A book about growth should be exactly
about that, growth. Ask yourself, how can my book help
someone grow? How can my story affect people out
there? Most of the people who will read your book are
not interested in your life as much as you'd think. They

are however interested in how you bested unfortunate circumstances, and the steps you took. My point is research your conflict and find the solutions. Your help to others is not by telling them what to do but merely suggesting this is what worked for me. Everyone's struggle is different.

Format is an essential piece to having a good book. Placing the right information into the best chapter or scene will help deliver the impact your story can have. Essentially this is comparable to a house built with bricks. You have to lay out the format of how that house will be developed. One would need to know how the bricks will stack amongst each other to stand strong and withstand intake. That intake for you will be the criticism that will inevitably come. Formatting can create a decent setting and help depict the perfect and vivid picture your words can compose.

2. Articles
Read as many articles (of the millions that are out there) about character development, plot construction, and relativity. There are so many articles that can teach you how to introduce your character(s).

And even more articles on how to develop them throughout your story.

Find what works for you. You can only tell what you can prove. Your writing will be a direct reflection of how you reach your audience. Go to the library, and then make a list of all the books you picked up related to your message. Go home and then research the topics involved. Of course, you are going to come across articles that say do this, and another will say do that. However, do whatever you feel is going to bring the best out of your project. Your book is your book and it will only turn out exactly how you determine. Articles are a good source for learning how to be more DIY. As a matter of fact, some articles or forums will actually have reviews and comments. Read them as well, and you should do this because this will help determine how you should perceive or take the information.

3. Read

Find any book like the one you are composing and read it. I know you might fear the idea of plagiarism. Well, trust me, no good or great author didn't. But, the most significant thing to realize is "All great artist copy."

Remember, you aren't the first to do it and you will not be the last. Never take anyone's work word for word. That is for sure plagiarism. Instead, take note to the structure in which they used to develop their story and characters. Get a feel for how their story flows. This will increase your chances of writing a story as compelling if not more.

Don't fear, you will still have the opportunity to have your own style.

After you have researched, continue writing. Create and complete your story. And then, read over it. As insane as this may sound, read over your story at least twenty times. Keep reading until you feel comfortable with what you have.

When you are done you will now have the terrible yet necessary task of revision. Trust me, this part sucks but it is worth it. Unless, you have super marketing skills. But, we will talk about that later. You will need an editor. Yes, an editor. Those people who will crucify your work as they rip your story to shreds with their opinion of errors. Criticism will be rough. Believe me. However, do not let it defeat you. You can counter this process by learning the editorial process yourself. Again, read more articles. Figure out what mistakes you can correct and what writing style you want. The phrase goes, *"why pay someone to do what you can teach yourself how to do?"*

After you have done this, now you will need a **Focus Group**. This will be a group of individuals who have no relation or association with you whatsoever. These people can be people you know but not personally. The reason for this is because they are going to be your test subjects. Pick about five people and develop about ten questions about your book.

How did you like the book?
What didn't you like about the book?
Were you able to connect with the characters?
Did you have trouble understanding what the conflict was?
Did the story pick up slow or right away?
Did you like the ending?

Would you recommend this book?
Would you read it again?

Etc...

Give your test readers about a week. A full week, literally seven days. Don't call them like that scary chick in the movies and whisper it to them. Simply give them a goal time, and then request their feedback.

5/5 - You're ready
4/5 - One bad review won't stop the show
3/5 - Go back and look over what concerned the two and determine if it needs to be changed, or, what can be changed.
2/5 - Your book really needs work, go back to the drawing board and get to work.
1/5 - Give up. No just kidding. Your story may be premature and need a lot of fixing.

After you are deemed ready, next you need to determine how you want to publish. Here is where the marketing comes in.
I'll be honest, even a bad book can sell. All you have to

do is know how to market. If you ignore any information in this book, do not ignore this. Reader, marketing is any key essential move to having any success. You cannot control the market because it fluctuates frequently. However, you can control how often you are on the market. Before I get there, let's talk about just a few more things.

Ok...But how do we publish?

There are two ways to publish.

Traditional

Create a query letter. Create a synopsis. And send both off to literary agencies.

QUERY LETTER

These questions are extremely important and I am sure you are asking why? Well because of "Query letters." This is a piece of information in letter format that will explain the following:

- What your book is?
- Why is your book important?

- What makes your book so special?
- Why will your book sell?

A query letter is one of the most challenging obstacles to publishing a book. Some might say that a query letter is only necessary if you plan on publishing traditionally. I'll get to that type of publishing later. However, a query letter can be useful to you just as much as anyone else. You can learn about your project by simply drafting one. I recommend that you try to establish a query letter before you even write your book. Before you write one consider your audience. Think about what they would like to hear and how you would pitch your book to them. As a result, having a well put together query can also help you develop an amazing pitch. This pitch can also be the verbatim response to in-person inquiry of your novel. Take into consideration that when giving your book to an agent or simply to a potential business partner, you want them to acknowledge how unique and profound your work is. Yet, that same reaction is what you want from your potential readers in person.

You can google to find an agent and there will be

different agencies that work with your target genre. Read their site carefully and always following their instructions. These people are fickle. TRUST ME. FOLLOW THEIR INSTRUCTIONS! If they say they want you to double space, make every first word italic, and send in your query with reading glasses and coffee. Then you do that. They have a distinct process in which they undergo selecting authors. You don't want to ruin your chance by not listening. Also, flood their emails. Trust me some agent is reading this and is crunching their teeth, balling a fist, and waiting for their chance to punch me in the face. But, so what, I can fight. So anyway, flood their emails with your best query. Send in a query and wait for a response. If you are denied, revise your query and send it in again. Repeat until they simply respond with frustration or an acceptance notice. But these are people who believe they want guaranteed success. They are not interested in making a career for anyone who does not already have one. This is why I dislike these people but I respect their career. And in the same sense I love them. Your focus should be to be noticed.

Publishing with an agent will undergo a few processes. First you have to convince an agent to sell your book to a publishing house. (Not easy but possible) Most agents pick up already endorsed writers. Meaning, someone can vouch for your book. Once they sell your book, you will get a barely convincing advance. A few thousand dollars, which if you know best you will utilize for marketing. Then, the publishing company will provide distribution, which is the mass benefit of going the agency route. Your book will be placed all over the country wherever it can sell in bookstores.

It may seem at first like this is the long and hard way to become a successful author. Um, well yeah it is. However, this process can be extremely rewarding. You will have the distribution channels on lock. Having distribution is possibly the type rope most can walk with confidence. The upside is you really only have to market your book. Gain exposure and where your book can be found. And, it will be there. Your agent will make sure of that. There are perks to being a published author in the big named community of major publishing houses. So while I might frown upon them, I actually encourage you to try this method. Go for it.

Self-publish

Basically, act without a major publisher and do all the legwork yourself.

There are benefits to both. Regardless of each, in both processes you will have to market your work yourself. You need to be promoting your book at least 6 months to a year before you release it. And agents require you to have an established following. Which means promote yourself!

So, in this case you need to find your audience. If you are writing a romance novel, you don't want to advertise it to a Star Wars fanatic. Find the people who will be interested in your book and tell them about it. You will have to talk to people so I hope being shy isn't your thing. Connect with everyone who has any correlation to your book. If you are writing a book about World War 2, then it's in your best interest to seek out active individuals in the military and veterans, or anyone who has family in the military. The goal is to bring awareness about your book. The number one reason books do not sell is because no one has any idea that the book is even in existence.

Follow blogs, fans, and go through comments on articles about any topic that correlates to your book. Join organizations that have people who will be affected by your story.

Whether you try to get published by a major publishing house or self-publish, they both require an audience.

If you do seek an agent, heads up, this process is long and drawn out. And royalty rates are beyond discomforting. The industry just is not what it used to be. There won't be any super advance where you are getting a book deal for $100k up front. Barely any double digit thousand dollar advances will be in sight, unless you are a celebrity with a following already. And even they don't see that much anymore.

Now, if you self-publish, your only setback is that you will not have that distribution support immediately. Instead, your book will be print in demand. Which means, it will not be developed until purchased. At most you'll have an online market set up free of charge, but you have to do all the legwork. Now it is possible to get your book in stores. Difficult but possible. Choose who you publish with wisely. If anyone charges you to publish your book then RUN LIKE HELL. These are not people you want to associate with. They will leave you high and dry.

Amazon offers Createspace, who will publish your book for free. A good opportunity but the stipulation is most stores won't buy your book. Createspace does not offer "buy back" which basically the store is able to return books they can't sell back to you, or the publisher. And most book buyers steer away from independent authors. The loop hole around this is to buy your own **ISBN**. If you asked what the heck that is, well, you should stop and familiarize yourself with the term. No book is purchased without one. Buying your own ISBN will permit you to list your book as whoever you desire to be the publisher. Most book buyers are going for sure shots, but if you have a convincing cover and a convincing publishing name, there is a major shot at landing your book in stores. You cannot use the same ISBN twice. Do not try to do that, instead save your money and make a budget for your project that includes the cost of your ISBN. One ISBN will cost you $125. Be mindful that some publishers who will allow you to self-publish will offer an ISBN for you, but under their own terms and conditions. If you want full control, my recommendation is that you buy the ISBN yourself and then go from there. This can be a tricky process but you will succeed.

There are other companies who offer buy back so dig around, like Ingramspark. You can still get your book in stores, but it depends on how you approach it. Always offer buy back, and always have a sales pitch. How much can you guarantee will sell? What are your sales projections?

Honestly, having an audience is key. When you know your audience you can provide more proof of your progress.

With self-publishing, your book is essentially your business. You are legit a business owner. All the legwork is your responsibility. But here is the best part. Your royalty percentage is at least 30% and higher. Which means you can really bank off your book if it sells. Whereas with traditional publishing you may make .66

cents off the dollar or poorly less, with SP you can make anywhere from $2-$5 off of your book. I'm sure you can do the math on that.

SP is also you spending a lot of your own money. But what's life without risk? Take a lot of risk! Don't put up your house as collateral of course, but be prepared to purchase advertising. Remember, people do not buy books they have no idea are being sold. The more exposure, the more awareness. The more awareness and the more sales.

<u>Notes</u>

Build your game plan

Either method can work but the most important factor is knowing the market. You want a large fan base so contact content creators, or digital media execs. These are people you will pay to get you real life active followers who are interested in your book. So we have finally reached the point where I share the secret no one ever tells you.

Buy into everything!

Think about it. People need to know your book is here. We live in a day and age where social media can make you a millionaire in minutes. But, you have to pay the piper. Here is what you do. Research all relevant fields of media i.e. The Shaderoom, Hollywood News, People, and etc. find popular YouTubers and Instagrammers and put your money where your mouth is. Most people buy anything from advertisements. Use the FB ad option. Utilize all the opportunities to advertise. Yes, this means spending a lot of your own money. So what! You will make it back. The community loves to make money off of you by making you money off of your audience, who then becomes your customers.

When you start to promote your business, content creators, online marketers, and so many people and businesses will reach out to you. The first thing you will do is say "They just want my money." Uh yea.

Pay them, and do this because these people know what they are doing and they know the business. They know exactly what you need and how to get you there. They just want to be paid for it like you do. Stop being scared to spend money. Find a good marketing strategy that puts your book in front of everyone.

You should be out at events passing out flyers and business cards. Also, give away as much as you can afford. Remember you are trying to find your audience, and in some cases you have to make your audience. Non-profit marketing is scary, especially if you paid for a service. In the end you have to focus on what exactly you are getting for your top dollar. Attention is key. Everyone should know about your book. Creating a web of resources can improve your chances of getting a response from people who can become your fan. Work hard. Study and determine if you truly want to get your story out there. Another big point is learn how to write a good LOG LINE. This is the shortest pitch for your book. It's the synopsis in only one or two sentences. Next, you need a slogan. Think of something crafty that people don't mind repeating.

Throughout your journey many questions and non-believers will share their distaste. Fortunate for you I am here to warn you that it is up to you to establish a good defense against negativity and establish a tolerance for rejection. You will hear a lot of no's. That is part of the path. Do not stray because you heard no one too many times. Instead, use that last no to power your drive to hear the first yes. You can do this and I know because anyone can do it. Your story is compelling but you need to make sure you can tell it in a way that it captivates. Trust in yourself and believe in your past and journey. Accept who you are and accept who you were. And then, move on. Show the world that what you have been through will not define you but empower you to be better.

At all cost, write. It is the only way you will ever become an advanced writer. Also, if one editor does not like your book, move on. Everything is not for everyone. Believe in yourself. And make time to write. No matter what. You got this!

<u>The End</u>

That wraps up this book. I told you it would not be long. However, trust me, what I just told you is really expensive. Someone out there will try and sell you this information for a lot of money. Never forget to educate yourself. If there is anything I can leave you with just know that I want you to learn as much as possible. So your journey can be a focused effort directing you into your potential.

I have to go now, my life is in an incredible bad shape. And I haven't had coffee in days. Possibly weeks, and maybe longer. Oh God...

I hope this helps for now. There is a lot to this industry but if you want my advice. Self-publish and run your own show.

If you want to know anything else just email me. Have a

blessed career and I wish you well.

Sincerely,

Christian Cole

Message to the Best

I want to let you know that nothing comes easy. But, success can come from smart choices and realizing that you do have a choice. Be mindful that your journey is not over. Focus on your goals and always plan your week ahead. You can make a great difference in your life and others by sharing your story. You are loved and you are appreciated. I believe in you and all I need you to do now is believe in yourself. YOU GOT THIS! You are probably looking for my email. Well follow me and you got it!

c.d_colemanbooks_ via **Instagram**
Thats_Cori via **Twitter**

Ps.

Eat Tacos, tacos make people happy.

Ich entschuldige mich für alles, was ich getan habe. Ich habe nie gefühlt Liebe und ich versuchte mein Bestes, um etwas, das ich nicht fühlen konnte geben.
Verzeih mir

www.ingramcontent.com/pod-product-compliance
Lightning Source LLC
Chambersburg PA
CBHW040346060426
42445CB00029B/20